Ava Antibody Explains

Your Body and Vaccines

Written by Andrea Cudd Alemanni

Illustrated by Roman Diaz

Ava Antibody Explains

Published by Wisdom House Books, Inc.
Chapel Hill, North Carolina 27514 USA • 1.919.883.4669
www.wisdomhousebooks.com
Wisdom House Books is committed to excellence in the publishing industry.
Book design copyright © 2020 by Wisdom House Books, Inc.
All rights reserved.

Cover and Interior Illustration by Roman Diaz
Cover and Interior design by Ted Ruybal
Published in the United States of America
Hardback ISBN: 978-1-7334210-0-3
LCCN: 2020907294

JNF051050 | JUVENILE NONFICTION / Science & Nature / Biology
JNF051000 | JUVENILE NONFICTION / Science & Nature / General
HEA050000 | HEALTH & FITNESS / Vaccinations

First Edition

25 24 23 22 21 20 / 10 9 8 7 6 5 4 3 2 1

Disclaimer:

Ava Antibody Explains: Your Body and Vaccines is an educational tool for young children intended to help them understand the purpose of vaccines. This book is not a substitute for medical advice and can hopefully facilitate communication with your healthcare professionals.

This book is dedicated to

Linda Saunders Cudd:
My loving and talented mother who provided concept sketches of Ava Antibody nearly twenty years ago.

Ashley Alemanni and William Alemanni:
My children and inspiration for book characters, but more importantly, for my life.

Mark Grunenwald:
My life partner and unwavering supporter of my entrepreneurial spirit.

Scientists and physicians developing vaccines and providing evidence of their safety.

A portion of the proceeds from this book will be donated to the Rotary International polio vaccination initiative for children, End Polio Now. Over the last 30 years, Rotarians have worked tirelessly with partner organizations, travelling to remote areas of the world to protect children from this paralyzing and potentially deadly virus. At this writing, Rotary has donated more than 1.8 billion US dollars to eradicate polio.

When you are at the doctor,
she may say you need a shot.
It can be scary or even hurt a little.
You may wonder,

Why do I need this?

Let's find out together!

First, you need to meet

Ava Antibody!

She is going to show you how getting shots helps you stay healthy and happy.

Ava is on a team in your body called the immune system. Their job is to patrol your body and find anything that isn't supposed to be there.

They find things you can see,
like a splinter.

They also find things you can't see,
like germs and viruses,
such as this guy–

Charlie Chickenpox.

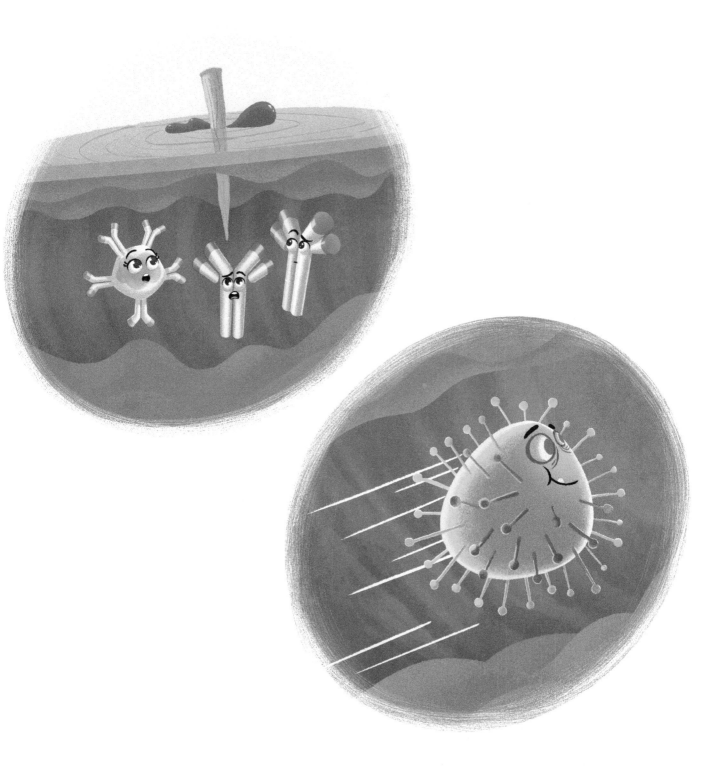

However, Charlie Chickenpox
is very sneaky!

If the immune system doesn't know
what he looks like, Charlie can get
right past them.

If Charlie Chickenpox gets into your
body, he can make you sick and give
you itchy, blotchy red spots!

Once the team has met
Charlie Chickenpox, they know what
to look for and will sound the alarm!

Then the immune system can
band together and get rid of him.

This is Will.
He has never had Charlie Chickenpox
before, so Ava doesn't know what
to look for.

What do you think
happens now?

"Since Ava doesn't know who I am, I can make this little boy have Chickenpox. But, she will remember me. I only have one chance to make Will sick!"

Charlie Chickenpox snuck right by Ava, and now Will doesn't look so good, does he?

He has a fever and yucky, itchy red bumps. Will can't go to school or play with his friends for days!

Ava can see Charlie Chickenpox now, so she sounds the alarm for the rest of her team to get rid of him.

"Now that I know what to look for, Charlie Chickenpox can't sneak by me anymore! I will be able to spot him quickly, and he can't get Will sick!"

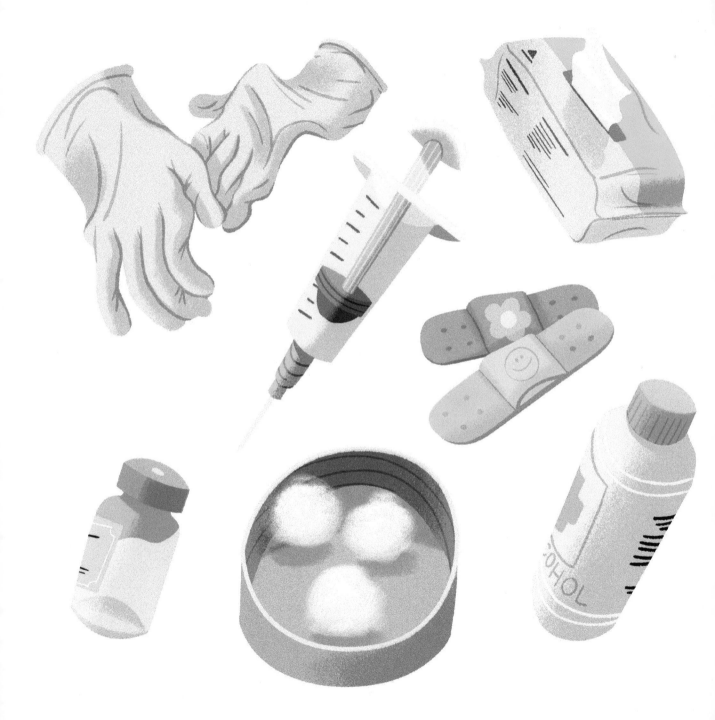

Good news!

Charlie Chickenpox doesn't have to get you sick. Ava just has to know what to look for. Your doctor can teach her with a special trick: shots!

Doctors give you a shot because it has a special kind of Charlie Chickenpox in it. The shot helps Ava know what Charlie looks like. This way, she can sound the alarm and stop you from getting sick when he tries to make a home in YOUR body. Another word for a shot is "vaccine."

This is Ashley.
She had the Chickenpox vaccine
last year.

Even though Charlie Chickenpox
tried to make her sick, he couldn't!

Why not?

It's because Ava Antibody knows what Charlie Chickenpox looks like, and she can be on the lookout for him.

She and her team can stop Charlie from making Ashley sick!

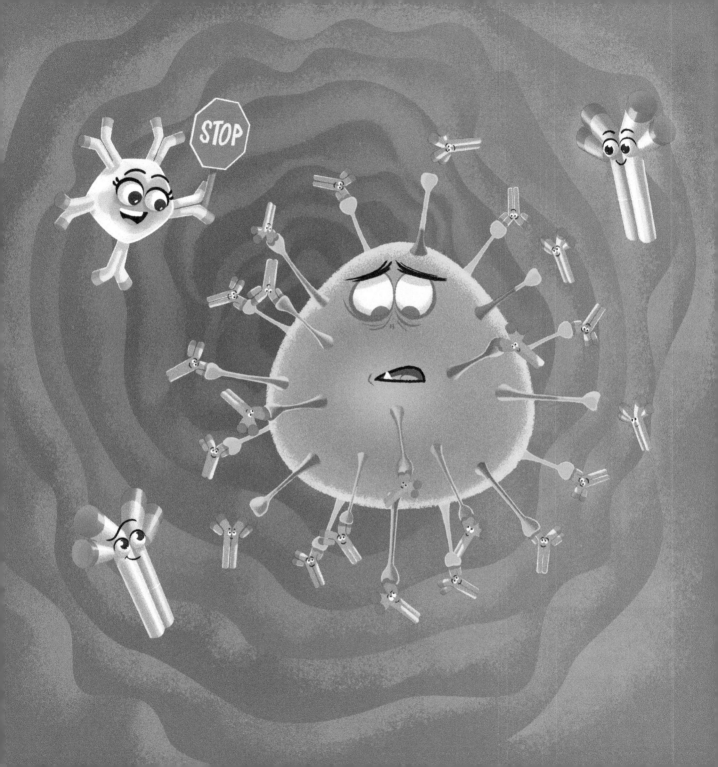

Getting the vaccine helps you
keep your friends healthy, too!

Amara is friends with Ashley.
Her baby brother is too young to
get the shot. If Ashley got sick with
Charlie Chickenpox, he could easily
spread to Amara's brother, too!

Ava Antibody is happy
to keep you healthy!

It's her favorite job.

The Immune System

A World Within Us We Train with Vaccinations

Our immune system is a complicated network of responses that are active every second of every day, even without our awareness. When working properly, our bodies can attack foreign invaders using multiple processes. However, with this level of complexity, offering children and parents an educational tool about the benefits of vaccines is no easy task. This book addresses the immune system's response to administered vaccinations, remaining as accurate and basic as possible.

Ava describes the B-cell's role in initiating an immune response when exposed to a virus or vaccine. Once activated by the presence of an antigen, the B-cells produce antibodies. Just like Ava, they recognize the antigen and bind to its surface. This prevents the virus from invading healthy cells and reproducing or replicating, therefore preventing illness. Once antibodies are present, you could be exposed to a virus and remain healthy for months or years to come.

The history of vaccine development has centered on one main objective: provide the body with safe exposure to a pathogen before infection with the fully potent disease. Amazingly, this concept was being utilized to fight the deadly smallpox virus before germ theory was proven by Louis Pasteur and Robert Koch in the 1860s.

Vaccines are safer today than ever before. While there are risks, they should always be weighed against the benefits. Vaccinating your child protects them and others who cannot get vaccinated or are immune compromised.

And yet, even with the availability and supply of vaccines, outbreaks still occur. These outbreaks are generally caused by the breakdown of protection offered by "herd immunity." If a high percentage of the population is vaccinated, an antigen can be introduced without many illnesses. Those who are vaccinated will be exposed, but their bodies will not replicate the virus. Only a small number of people will get sick, and the outbreak will be contained.

However, if a population of largely unvaccinated people come into contact with the virus, it will spread rapidly, and there will be no "herd immunity" to protect the vulnerable members.

As your child's advocate, it is your responsibility to make informed decisions and rely on trustworthy sources. The Centers for Disease Control and Prevention (CDC) has informative videos and materials about vaccinations for children and adults. The Food and Drug Administration (FDA) describes the process by which vaccine safety is determined. And of course, the National Institutes of Health (NIH) and your health care provider can assist you with additional resources and information.

Vaccinations are heralded as one of the most important medical advancements in history and with good cause! Vaccines arm the individual and the masses with protection which can otherwise be gained only through suffering the actual illness.

For additional information, resources, and recommendations, please see:

Bill and Melinda Gates Foundation. https://www.gatesfoundation.org/

Centers for Disease Control and Prevention. https://www.cdc.gov/

"Coronavirus, Explained." *Netflix*, 2020.

U.S. Food and Drug Administration. https://www.fda.gov/

Haelle, Tara. *Vaccination Investigation; The History and Science of Vaccines*. Twenty-First Century Books, 2018.

Murin, Charles D., Wilson, Ian A., and Andrew B. Ward. "Antibody Responses to Viral Infections: A Structural Perspective Across Three Different Enveloped Viruses." *Nature Microbiology*, 2019 May; 4(5): 734-747.

National Institutes of Health. https://www.nih.gov/

"Mayo Clinic Q+A Podcasts with Dr. Gregory Poland, a Mayo Clinic Infectious Diseases Expert." *Mayo Clinic*, 2020.

Offit, Paul. *Bad Advice: Or Why Celebrities, Politicians and Activists Aren't Your Best Source of Health Information*. Columbia University Press, 2018.

Rotary International. *End Polio*. https://www.endpolio.org/

"Vaccine Education Center." *Children's Hospital of Philadelphia*. https://www.chop.edu/centers-programs/vaccine-education-center

ABOUT THE AUTHOR

Andrea Cudd Alemanni

Andrea is a life-long resident of North Carolina, with a chemistry degree from Appalachian State University. As a child, she remembers mixing powders and shampoos together to observe changes in color and consistency. Andrea has been known to dissect caterpillars or chicken hearts and keep insects in the freezer to educate her children. She has always believed adolescents can understand much more about science and their bodies if provided with comprehensible explanations. She takes pride in working as a liaison between experts and the general public trying to make sense of science. This niche, along with her interest in biology and medicine, poised Andrea to become an independent patient advocate and founder of Patient Navigation Team, LLC.

When she's not engaging in scientific research, Andrea enjoys volunteering, supporting arts education, and spending time with her family. She resides in Summerfield and has two adult children, Ashley and Will.

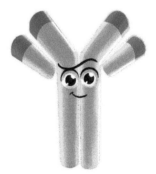

ABOUT THE ILLUSTRATOR

Roman Diaz

Roman is from Mexico and was born and raised in the city of Toluca. His first drawings were for schoolwork, where he enjoyed copying photos and cartoons. Years later, he majored in graphic design and found that children's illustration fulfilled him as an artist. His work is full of vibrant colors, and he aims to evoke emotional responses from his audiences.

Roman is the recipient of several awards for his designs and advertising in Mexico, including Best Mobile Game in VJMX 2019 for Ghost Attack. He has worked for Nick Jr. creating character designs for children's shows. In his free time, he enjoys spending time with family and friends and travelling around his beautiful country. He currently works and resides in Mexico City.

History Repeats Itself

We have witnessed in real time the devastating effects of a disease for which we have essentially no defense. Until a vaccine is readily available, society must rely on the same principles that saved lives during the Spanish flu (1918): closing businesses and eliminating social gatherings. This tragedy has laid before us the indisputable fact that vaccinations save lives and save economies from near ruin.

In addition, with outbreaks of preventable childhood diseases occurring around the world, the World Health Organization (WHO) considered vaccine hesitancy to be one of "Ten Threats to Global Health in 2019." That's right up there with climate change, HIV, and flu pandemic (for which there is NO vaccine).

When considering where this hesitancy comes from, I thought back to my experience in taking my own children to the doctor for shots. I do not recall any explanation of vaccine benefits. I was handed a sheet of paper, my child was poked in the leg, and off I went with a crying kid! I drafted this book to change that paradigm. With my mother, Linda Saunders Cudd as illustrator, *Ava Antibody* was brought to life. I address the controversial topic of vaccines in the inaugural book of my children's health education series—why start anywhere else?

Now **you** can provide your child with an explanation of vaccines that they will understand. *Ava Antibody Explains: Your Body and Vaccines* is a valuable educational tool, introducing children to the immune system and how vaccines aid in preventing sickness. Ava even explains herd immunity! This book provides a true inside look at how vaccinations defend the body against illness without having to endure the illness itself.

Ava will have many more adventures inside the body! Feel free to offer suggestions for more topics in the series at www.avaantibody.com.

CPSIA information can be obtained
at www.ICGtesting.com
Printed in the USA
BVHW091728160522
637152BV00001B/1